SKETCHES AROUND FOWEY

Published by Dyllansow Truran, Croft Prince, Mount Hawke,
Truro, Cornwall TR48EE
Printed by R. Booth at the Troutbeck Press, Antron Hill, Mabe,
Penryn, Cornwall TR109HH
ISBN 1 85022 139 1 (cased) ISBN 1 85022 140 5 (paperback)

walked to Gribbeu Head on a sunny Autumn day,
Wonderful views back to Polruau, Fowey hidden behind
Lankelly cliff, & the river snaking inland

FOR THE SAFETY OF COMMERCE
AND
FOR THE PRESERVATION OF MARINERS
THIS BEACON WAS ERECTED IN THE YEAR OF OUR LORD 1832
BY THE CORPORATION OF TRINITY HOUSE OF DEPTFORD STROND
THE MOST NOBLE JOHN JEFFREYS PRATT MARQUIS CAMDEN K.G. MASTER
CAPT. JOHN WOOLMORE KCH DEPUTY MASTER

Notice over the Daymark door

But once you reach The Daymark its hard to draw it! It needs to
be seen from the distance . . .

an enamel
colander

A 'Beachcombers' paradise.
' nets & chains ' floats & buoys,
au old 'lobster' pot & a
grappling hook,
scythes!

plastic
floats
& cork
shells & stones.

footpath

FARTHINGS
at Readymoney

4

I must find out what the collective noun for Jackdaws is - whatever it is it just flew by! Dozens of them . .

Early morning - v sunny but COLD. Boys digging bait - I'm going for coffee

5

It's very hard to see Fowey from the land. You have to go on the river to see its narrow streets & steep hillside.

6

From here you can see the narrow lane, between river & hill, leading from the original ferry crossing to the old town.

The older streets are narrow & shaded - sunlight slanting in across the rooves

8

I overheard a conversation, sitting here in the sun on a December day – "I wouldn't live down the other end if you paid me. The wind always blows down Passage Street."

Its true! it does...

whereas on the Esplanade the houses are huge & ornate bright white & pastel colours reflecting the sun. Windows, balconies, gables, every decorative device plastered on. Open aspects, river views – what a different way of life. Of course, I prefer the tiny houses huddled around the quays, their back doors on the river – safe in the shadow of the church – cold & damp too!. years ago...

9

'Peudennick'

When one of these big boats left the other evening, in the dark, lights on board shining; there were shouts of 'goodbye' from the ferry slip & men waving & calling from the deck...

I love to watch the tugs working. The very big boats come in stern first, with a tug at each end.

'Tregeagle'

River traffic - fishing boats going out early
& back late. Sturdy little open boats
carrying the men who keep the harbour
working.
Tugs & ferries.
Tatty coasters & shiny, smart yachts

even the schoolchildren get ferried across each morning
from Bodinnick to Caffa Mill in a little open boat or the ferry)

The Polruan Ferryman

HARBOUR PATROL

Drizzly rain

The river is a perfect blend (for me)
between the picturesque & the hardworking.

But it takes more than that to put the
fishermen off.

13

coffee & a view of Polruan

A Saturday morning in Fowey

14

The shadow of a tree in the churchyard looks
as if it's been painted on the house wall.

The centre of town - old houses, shops
& alleyways clustered around the
church

15

The Pilot boat

A BIG boat

The thing that fascinates me about the Fowey is how busy it is...
It never stops.
You wake in the night to the noise of engines, r look out to see a HUGE
boat passing.   The docks are never empty.   Boats slowly sink
lower in the water as they load up with china clay.   A mist of it
rises over the boat - - - r ends up on my car in the car park
                              which turns a subtle shade of grey!

The boats come from all over ---   Russia, Germany,
Spain, Norway, even Britain...! I had no idea so much china clay
          was used

The Polruan Ferry

The Bodinnick Ferry goes back & forth
all day from first light to dusk. It
carries the school children, mini buses
& ambulances as well as cars.
Some days, when it's blowing hard & the tide is running
it has quite a struggle.... On calmer days the swans swim alongside
to be fed scraps from the "driver's?" lunch.... And they keep up!

A very peculiar thing to draw - just a raft with a boat alongside

Little gulls flying up river

7.45am very cold. white frost on hills. tatten of mist blowing like smoke on the water.

9am. mist still blowing along the water

11am sun lighting the tops of trees - Tide High

12.30 strong shadows, tide falling. still cold

.45pm Pinker, softer light.

3pm No shadows, strong, low light · colder

.30pm. light fading fast

5.80pm Nearly dark. Tide rising.

5pm.ish – the little gulls, hundreds of them fly, low over the water, downing to roost

19

Golant — a lovely house right on
the water. unlived in &
neglected, but what a
beautiful spot. (& wet.)

Beware
road liable to be
flooded at
high tide.

20

The tide coming in fast under the railway bridge – I waited, but didn't see a train...

21

A tatty old shed . . . . with lovely curtains!

And a camouflaged postbox

POST OFFICE

E R

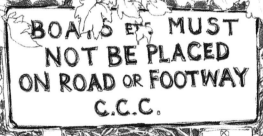

Sculptural junk is ok though......

23

Lostwithiel - an old-fashioned town...
interesting shops, like stepping back in time.

The river here is neither tumbling & small as it is upstream nor
does it seem salty & strong & tidal as it does further down. It seems
a place quite apart...

Spring blossom

LANHYDROCK · · ·

Lanhydrock
Walking through the Autumn leaves down to the house
Dappled sun & slanting shadows. Very quiet & still

27

the front of the House . . . . . .
Sunny & bright — Imposing & formal.

And the back...
Dark & shadowy. All odd-shaped rooves & chimneys. I actually feel more at home here... I'd have been a servant in a previous life... Not the Lady of the house.

Respryn Bridge. Had to climb a fence & scramble
down a bank into MUD to get this view
(watched by curious cows :-)

30

Then walked awhile along the river. Little paths, roots, trees & dappled sun. Disturbed for a few seconds by the sound of the Paddington to Penzance train rushing by completely hidden by the trees. From the train you'd never guess this place existed . . .

St. Winnow. - A tiny hamlet of church, a few houses & barns,
Right on the river at the end of
what seems like miles of narrow, twisty
lanes.

just follow the cream teas sign —
its worth it...

The blocked up archway in the barn is all
that remains of an old manor house

STNN
LOSTWITHIEL 2
LERRYN 2
IMPRACTICABLE FOR CARS

looking across from the church.
The railway line to Fowey on the far side
of the river.

33

Reflections at Lerryn — still + quiet

34

The tide creeping in on a Sunday afternoon – slowly covering the road – I'm not sure if I should wake the couple in their car up, or if the banging of the other car doors will do it...

..... Time to go & rescue more anyway...

35

36

A day spent watching the tide
dropping & the mud appearing,
chatting to the builders —
amateur painters all, the
dustman, who works in pen &
ink & looking at old photos
produced by a man from one
of the cottages. A perfect day.

This shed was used years ago by the grandfather of a man in one of the nearby cottages, to store his scrumpy

Lerryn is such a pretty place — the car just seems to come here of its own accord — I don't mean to! I think — "I'll just sit & look at the river for a minute or two" — & here I am . . . .

The stepping stones are guarded by a very large Muscovey Drake

And I don't like the way he's looking at me...

39

This is the view that says Bodinnick to me.... sitting in the window at Ferrymans cottage, coffee in hand, watching the ferry come & go, the little harbour boats pass & the pilot boat & big boats going to the Docks. At night the lights reflect off the water & big boats still slide by with a steady thump of engines......

40

Ferryside in winter — I'm sure it looks wonderful in the summer, but on a late January afternoon with strong shadows & pinks & red ochres in the trees it is glorious. The gulls flash white as they turn to catch the sun.

41

The bridge & old mill at Pearps — & over the bridge an orchard. There is a
cider for sale notice on a
Farm gate just up the road.

very good it was too.

so pen tips in
cider apples.

NOTICE

Dues for discharging or shipping over these quays will be collected as follows,

Grain 1ᵖ per Quarter
Timber 3ᵈ per Load.
Manures 3ᵈ per Ton.
Sand 2ᵈ Coal 3ᵈ

Other goods in like proportion.

Wᵐ PEASE
Steward.

Dated Lostwithiel May 10ᵗʰ 1894."

Pont - just a few houses hidden away in a steep, wooded valley. The notice above is still on the wall of one of the houses. Its hard to believe that these quays were once that busy.

The 'Bone Gull'

A regular visitor to Scilly - strange to see her tied up here & not floating peacefully in Lawrence's Bay at Home.

43

44

...wan is all hill ......
... it feels all UP hill to me!
But its worth it.
The views are wonderful.

Public Footpath
The Cliffs ½

Public Footpath
The Hills ¼

(even when it pours with rain
just as you get to the top!)

I really like the simplicity
of this sign....

45

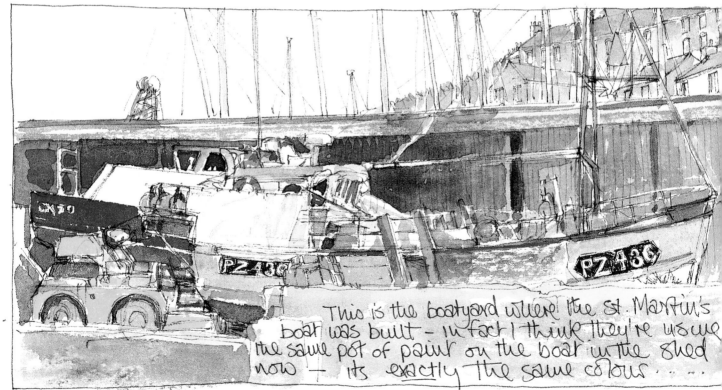

This is the boatyard where the St. Martin's boat was built — in fact I think they're using the same pot of paint on the boat in the shed now — its *exactly* the same colour......

46

Polruan
from Reg & Gladys' seat on the Esplanade
at Fowey.

47

.. And back to the beginning, crossing from Polruan on the ferry.
The Blockhouse & St. Catherines castle guarding the entrance to the
river & the Daymark in the distance... And i don't want to leave.....